THE ULTIMATE GUIDE TO REPAIR YOUR CREDIT

www.rangercreditrepair.com

JOHN MOORE

CONTENTS

Introduction:

In today's society, credit is an essential component that plays a significant role in various aspects of our lives. Whether it is purchasing a home, a car, or even getting a job, your credit score is often the deciding factor. A high credit score indicates that you are responsible with your finances and can manage your debts well. On the other hand, a low credit score can lead to various financial challenges, including high-interest rates, difficulty in getting loans or credit cards, and even rejection of job applications.

If you have a poor credit score, it can be a daunting task to repair it. That is where Ranger Credit Repair comes in. Ranger Credit Repair is a professional credit repair service that can help you repair your credit score quickly and efficiently. In this book, we will explore how Ranger Credit Repair can help you fix your credit score, the benefits of having a good credit score, and how you can maintain your credit score in the long run.

In conclusion, repairing your credit score can be a challenging but essential task. With the help of professional credit repair services, such as Ranger Credit Repair, and proper financial management, you can improve your credit score and secure a better financial future. We hope this book has provided you with the necessary information and resources to take the first steps towards repairing your credit score.

CHAPTER 1: UNDERSTANDING YOUR CREDIT SCORE

Your credit score is a crucial component of your financial health. It is a numerical representation of your creditworthiness and is used by lenders, landlords, and other financial institutions to determine if you are a reliable borrower. In this chapter, we will provide an overview of what a credit score is, how it is calculated, and the factors that influence your credit score.

What is a Credit Score?

A credit score is a three-digit number that ranges from 300 to 850 and is based on information from your credit report. The higher your credit score, the more trustworthy you appear to lenders, which can result in better loan terms and interest rates. Your credit score is calculated using various factors, including your payment history, credit utilization, length of credit history, and types of credit accounts.

How is a Credit Score Calculated?

Credit scoring models use complex algorithms to calculate your credit score. The most commonly used scoring model is the FICO score, which ranges from 300 to 850. The five main factors that influence your FICO score are:

Payment history: This factor accounts for 35% of your credit score and evaluates whether you have made payments on time.

Credit utilization: This factor accounts for 30% of your credit score and looks at the amount of credit you have available versus the amount you are using.

Length of credit history: This factor accounts for 15% of your credit score and evaluates how long you have been using credit.

Types of credit accounts: This factor accounts for 10% of your credit score and looks at the different types of credit accounts you have, such as credit cards, mortgages, and car loans.

Recent credit inquiries: This factor accounts for 10% of your credit score and evaluates how many new credit inquiries you have made.

Why is it Important to Monitor Your Credit Score?

Monitoring your credit score regularly is essential for several reasons. First, it allows you to detect any errors or fraudulent activity on your credit report, which can negatively impact your credit score. Second, it enables you to track your credit score over time and make adjustments to your financial habits accordingly. Third, it can help you identify areas where you need to improve your credit score, such as reducing your credit utilization or making payments on time.

How Can You Obtain a Free Credit Report?

Under federal law, you are entitled to one free credit report from each of the three major credit reporting agencies (Equifax, Experian, and TransUnion) every year. To obtain your free credit report, you can visit AnnualCreditReport.com, which is the only website authorized by the Federal Trade Commission to provide free credit reports. Alternatively, you can contact each credit reporting agency individually to request a free credit report.

Conclusion

Understanding your credit score is the first step towards repairing your credit. By monitoring your credit score regularly, you can detect errors or fraudulent activity and make adjustments to improve your credit score over time. In the next chapter, we will discuss in detail the different factors that influence your credit score and how to improve them.

CHAPTER 2: THE BENEFITS OF A GOOD CREDIT SCORE

A good credit score is essential for financial stability and opens up many opportunities for you. Lenders use your credit score to determine your creditworthiness and how much of a risk you pose to them. A higher credit score indicates that you are more likely to repay your debts on time, which makes you a less risky borrower. Here are some of the benefits of having a good credit score:

Lower Interest Rates

A good credit score can lead to lower interest rates on loans, credit cards, and mortgages. With a high credit score, lenders consider you less of a risk and are more likely to offer you lower interest rates. This can save you a significant amount of money in interest payments over the life of a loan.

Easier Loan Approvals

A good credit score can also increase your chances of getting approved for loans. When you apply for a loan, lenders review your credit report and score to determine if you are a reliable borrower. A higher credit score means you are more likely to be approved for loans and may qualify for higher loan amounts.

Better Credit Card Deals

Having a good credit score can also lead to better credit card deals, such as lower interest rates, higher credit limits, and more rewards. Credit card companies want to attract reliable borrowers, and a high credit score indicates that you are a low-risk borrower. This can lead to better credit card offers, such as cashback rewards, travel rewards, or lower annual fees.

Better Rental Opportunities

Landlords often review your credit score when considering your rental application. A good credit score can make you a more attractive tenant and increase your chances of getting approved for a rental property. Additionally, landlords may require a security deposit or co-signer if you have a low credit score, which can be avoided with a good credit score.

Lower Insurance Premiums

Some insurance companies use credit scores to determine the cost of insurance premiums. A good credit score can lead to lower insurance premiums, as insurance companies see you as a low-risk policyholder. This can save you money on car insurance, homeowner's insurance, and other types of insurance policies.

A good credit score is essential for financial stability and can lead to many benefits, including lower interest rates, easier loan approvals, better credit card deals, and better rental opportunities. By maintaining a good credit score, you can save money, increase your financial opportunities, and achieve financial stability. In the next chapter, we will discuss the different factors that impact your credit score and how to improve them.

CHAPTER 3: COMMON CREDIT REPORT ERRORS

Your credit report is an essential tool for lenders, employers, and landlords to assess your creditworthiness. It is vital that the information on your credit report is accurate to ensure that you receive the best possible interest rates and loan terms. Unfortunately, credit report errors are common, and they can negatively impact your credit score. In this chapter, we will discuss common credit report errors and what you can do to fix them.

Incorrect Personal Information

The first section of your credit report includes your personal information, such as your name, address, and social security number. Errors in this section are not uncommon, and they can be due to a typo or incorrect information provided by a lender or creditor. It is crucial to review this section carefully to ensure that all the information is correct.

Errors in Account Information

The account information section of your credit report includes all your credit accounts, including credit cards, loans, and mortgages. Errors in this section can include incorrect account balances, payment history, or even accounts that do not belong to you. These errors can significantly impact your credit score, so it is crucial to review this section carefully.

Inaccurate Public Record Information

Public records, such as bankruptcies, tax liens, and judgments, can also appear on your credit report. Errors in this section can include outdated or inaccurate information, which can negatively impact your credit score. It is essential to review this section carefully and dispute any errors promptly.

Identity Theft

Identity theft is a growing problem, and it can have a severe impact on your credit score. If you see accounts on your credit report that you do not recognize, it could be a sign of identity theft. It is crucial to dispute these accounts immediately and take steps to protect yourself from further harm.

What to Do if You Find an Error on Your Credit Report

If you find an error on your credit report, you should take action immediately. The first step is to contact the credit reporting agency and dispute the error. You should provide any supporting documents or information that can help resolve the issue.

Next, contact the lender or creditor associated with the error and inform them of the mistake. They should also correct the information with the credit reporting agency.

Finally, you should follow up with the credit reporting agency to ensure that the error has been corrected. It may take some time for the correction to appear on your credit report, so it is crucial to monitor your report regularly.

In conclusion, credit report errors are common, and they can have a significant impact on your credit score. It is essential to review your credit report regularly and dispute any errors promptly. By taking these steps, you can ensure that your credit report is accurate and improve your chances of obtaining favorable loan terms and interest rates.

CHAPTER 4: UNDERSTANDING CREDIT REPAIR

Credit repair is a process of identifying errors, inaccuracies, and negative items on your credit report and disputing them with credit reporting agencies. The goal of credit repair is to improve your credit score by removing negative items that are impacting your creditworthiness. Here are the basics of credit repair:

Identifying Errors and Negative Items

The first step in credit repair is identifying errors and negative items on your credit report. Negative items can include late payments, collections, charge-offs, bankruptcies, and judgments. It's important to review your credit report regularly to identify any inaccuracies or errors that may be impacting your credit score.

Disputing Inaccurate Information

Once you have identified inaccuracies or errors on your credit report, the next step is to dispute them with the credit reporting agencies. You can dispute errors or inaccuracies by writing a letter to the credit reporting agency explaining the error and providing any supporting documentation. The credit reporting agency must investigate your dispute within 30 days and remove any inaccurate information from your credit report.

Working with a Credit Repair Company

If you find the credit repair process overwhelming or don't have the time to manage it yourself, you can work with a credit repair company. A credit repair company can help you identify errors, dispute negative items, and improve your credit score. Ranger Credit Repair is a reputable credit repair company that can help you achieve financial stability by improving your credit score.

Credit repair is a process of identifying errors and negative items on your credit report and disputing them with credit reporting agencies. By working with a credit repair company like Ranger Credit Repair, you can improve your credit score and achieve financial stability. In the next chapter, we will discuss the importance of maintaining good credit habits and how to avoid credit pitfalls.

CHAPTER 5: THE BENEFITS OF PROFESSIONAL CREDIT REPAIR SERVICES

While you can attempt to repair your credit score on your own, hiring a professional credit repair service can provide you with many benefits. Here are some of the advantages of working with a reputable credit repair company like Ranger Credit Repair:

Expertise and Experience

Professional credit repair companies have the necessary expertise and experience to identify errors and inaccuracies on your credit report. They also have knowledge of the legalities involved in disputing negative items on your credit report. A credit repair company like Ranger Credit Repair has a team of experts who can handle the credit repair process efficiently and effectively.

Time-Saving

Credit repair can be a time-consuming process, especially if you are not familiar with the process. By working with a professional credit repair company, you can save time and focus on other important aspects of your life. The credit repair company will handle the dispute process and keep you updated on the progress.

Improved Credit Score

The main goal of credit repair is to improve your credit score. Professional credit repair services have the necessary resources and tools to dispute negative items on your credit report and improve your credit score. By working with a reputable credit repair company like Ranger Credit Repair, you can achieve a better credit score and financial stability.

Education and Guidance

Credit repair companies can also provide education and guidance on how to maintain good credit habits and avoid credit pitfalls. Ranger Credit Repair offers credit counseling and financial education to help clients achieve long-term financial success.

Hiring a professional credit repair service like Ranger Credit Repair can provide you with many benefits, including expertise, time-saving, improved credit score, and education. However, it's important to work with a reputable and trustworthy credit repair company to avoid scams and fraudulent activities. In the next chapter, we will discuss how to choose a reliable credit repair company.

CHAPTER 6: HOW RANGER CREDIT REPAIR WORKS

Ranger Credit Repair is a professional credit repair service that helps clients improve their credit scores by removing negative items from their credit reports. Here's how Ranger Credit Repair works:

Free Credit Report Consultation

The first step in the credit repair process with Ranger Credit Repair is a free credit report consultation. During the consultation, a credit specialist will review your credit report and identify any negative items that are bringing down your credit score.

Credit Report Analysis

After the consultation, Ranger Credit Repair will conduct a thorough credit report analysis to identify any errors or inaccuracies on your credit report. They will dispute any negative items that are incorrect, outdated, or unverifiable.

Credit Bureau Dispute Letters

Ranger Credit Repair will send credit bureau dispute letters to the credit reporting agencies on your behalf. These letters will outline the errors or inaccuracies in your credit report and request that they be removed.

Ongoing Communication

Throughout the credit repair process, Ranger Credit Repair will keep you updated on the progress of your case. They will also communicate with the credit reporting agencies and creditors to resolve any disputes or issues that arise.

Credit Counseling and Financial Education

In addition to credit repair services, Ranger Credit Repair also offers credit counseling and financial education. They provide clients with the knowledge and tools they need to maintain good credit habits and achieve long-term financial stability.

Services Offered by Ranger Credit Repair

Ranger Credit Repair offers a range of credit repair services to help clients achieve better credit scores, including:

Credit report analysis

Dispute letters to credit reporting agencies

Credit bureau communication and monitoring

Debt validation and negotiation

Credit counseling and financial education

Ranger Credit Repair works by identifying and disputing negative items on your credit report to improve your credit score. They offer a range of services to help clients achieve better credit scores and long-term financial success. In the next chapter, we will discuss how to choose a reliable credit repair company.

CHAPTER 7: THE COST OF CREDIT REPAIR SERVICES

Credit repair services can be a valuable investment for those looking to improve their credit scores, but they often come with a cost. In this chapter, we will explore the different pricing models of credit repair services and what to consider when choosing a service provider.

Types of Pricing Models

Credit repair services may use different pricing models, such as:

Monthly Subscription

Some credit repair services charge a monthly subscription fee for ongoing credit repair services. The fee may vary depending on the level of service you require.

Flat Fee

Other credit repair services may charge a flat fee for their services. This fee may be based on the number of negative items on your credit report or the complexity of your case.

Pay-per-Deletion

Pay-per-deletion is a pricing model where you pay only for the removal of negative items from your credit report. This pricing model is becoming more popular in the credit repair industry.

What to Consider When Choosing a Service Provider

When choosing a credit repair service, it's essential to consider the cost and the value you will receive. Here are some factors to consider when choosing a credit repair service:

Transparency and Ethics

Choose a credit repair company that is transparent about their services and fees. They should also follow ethical practices and comply with industry regulations.

Services Offered

Consider the services offered by the credit repair company and if they align with your needs. Some companies may offer additional services, such as credit counseling and financial education.

Cost

Compare the cost of services among different credit repair companies. Keep in mind that the cheapest option may not always be the best choice, and investing in a reputable credit repair company may save you money in the long run.

The cost of credit repair services varies depending on the pricing model and level of service you require. When choosing a credit repair service provider, consider their reputation, transparency, services offered, and cost. A reputable and trustworthy credit repair company can help you achieve your financial goals and improve your credit score.

CHAPTER 8: HOW LONG DOES CREDIT REPAIR TAKE?

If you're considering credit repair services, one of the most important questions you might have is how long it will take to improve your credit score. Unfortunately, there is no one-size-fits-all answer to this question, as the timeline for credit repair can vary depending on various factors.

The complexity of your case is one of the biggest factors that can influence how long credit repair takes. If you have multiple errors or negative items on your credit report, it may take longer to dispute and resolve each one. However, if your credit report has only a few errors or inaccuracies, the process may be quicker.

Another factor that can impact the duration of credit repair is your level of involvement. If you actively participate in the credit repair process by providing documentation and communicating with your credit repair company, the process can be quicker. On the other hand, if you are not proactive in providing the necessary information, the process may take longer.

It's important to keep in mind that credit repair is not an overnight process, and it may take several months to a year or more to see significant improvements in your credit score. This is because credit bureaus have 30 days to investigate disputes, and sometimes it can take several rounds of disputes to achieve the desired results.

Furthermore, if you have a history of delinquent payments, bankruptcy, or other major negative items on your credit report, it may take longer to see improvements in your credit score, even with credit repair services. However, with persistence and patience, you can see progress over time.

In summary, the timeline for credit repair can vary depending on several factors, including the complexity of your case, your level of involvement, and the extent of negative items on your credit report. While credit repair is not a quick fix, it can be a worthwhile investment in your financial future.

CHAPTER 9: MAINTAINING YOUR CREDIT SCORE

Congratulations! You have successfully repaired your credit score with the help of Ranger Credit Repair. Now, the next step is to maintain your credit score to ensure that you continue to enjoy the benefits of a good credit score.

Maintaining your credit score requires discipline and consistency. It is essential to understand the factors that influence your credit score and how to manage them effectively. Here are some tips to help you maintain your credit score:

Pay Your Bills on Time

Your payment history is one of the most critical factors that influence your credit score. Late payments can have a significant impact on your credit score, so it is essential to pay your bills on time. Set up automatic payments or reminders to ensure that you do not miss any payments.

Keep Your Credit Utilization Low

Credit utilization refers to the amount of credit you are using compared to your credit limit. High credit utilization can negatively impact your credit score, so it is essential to keep your credit utilization low. A good rule of thumb is to keep your credit utilization below 30%.

Monitor Your Credit Report Regularly

Monitoring your credit report regularly can help you identify any errors or fraudulent activities that may impact your credit score. You are entitled to a free credit report from each of the three major credit bureaus every year. Take advantage of this and review your credit report regularly.

Avoid Opening Too Many New Accounts

Opening too many new accounts in a short period can negatively impact your credit score. Every time you apply for credit, it results in a hard inquiry on your credit report, which can lower your score. Be mindful of how many accounts you open and how often you apply for credit.

Keep Old Accounts Open

The age of your credit accounts is another factor that influences your credit score. It is essential to keep old accounts open, even if you do not use them frequently. Closing old accounts can lower your credit score, so keep them open and use them occasionally to keep them active.

In conclusion, maintaining a good credit score requires discipline and consistency. Pay your bills on time, keep your credit utilization low, monitor your credit report regularly, avoid opening too many new accounts, and keep old accounts open. By following these tips, you can maintain a good credit score and enjoy the benefits that come with it.

CHAPTER 10: CREDIT COUNSELING SERVICES

Credit counseling services can be a valuable resource for individuals who are struggling with their finances and credit score. These services typically offer financial education and counseling to help individuals better understand their financial situation and create a plan to improve their credit score. In this chapter, we will explore the benefits of credit counseling services and how to choose a reputable service provider.

One of the primary benefits of credit counseling services is the access to professional financial advice. Credit counselors are trained professionals who can help you create a budget, manage your debt, and develop a plan to improve your credit score. They can also provide you with resources and education on financial management and credit score improvement.

Another benefit of credit counseling services is that they can negotiate with creditors on your behalf. If you are struggling to make payments on your debts, a credit counselor may be able to work with your creditors to negotiate a payment plan that is more manageable for you. This can help you avoid late fees, penalties, and other negative consequences of missed payments.

When choosing a credit counseling service provider, it is important to do your research and choose a reputable organization. Look for organizations that are accredited by reputable agencies such as the National Foundation for Credit Counseling (NFCC) or the Financial Counseling Association of America (FCAA). These organizations require their members to meet certain standards and adhere to a code of ethics.

It is also important to consider the cost of credit counseling services. Some organizations offer their services for free or at a low cost, while others may charge significant fees. Make sure you understand the pricing structure and any fees associated with the service before committing to a provider.

In conclusion, credit counseling services can be a valuable resource for individuals looking to improve their credit score and overall financial situation. These services offer professional financial advice, negotiation with creditors, and education on financial management. When choosing a service provider, it is important to do your research and choose a reputable organization that meets your needs and budget.

CHAPTER 11: IDENTITY THEFT AND CREDIT FRAUD

Identity theft and credit fraud are two of the most common financial crimes that can have a significant impact on your credit score and financial stability. Identity theft occurs when someone steals your personal information, such as your name, social security number, and credit card number, to commit fraud or other criminal activities. Credit fraud occurs when someone uses your credit card or other credit accounts to make unauthorized purchases or withdraw cash.

Detecting identity theft and credit fraud can be challenging, but there are warning signs to look out for. These signs include receiving bills for accounts you didn't open, unauthorized charges on your credit card or bank statements, and unexpected denials of credit applications. If you suspect that your identity has been stolen or your credit has been fraudulently used, it is essential to act quickly.

The first step to take when you suspect identity theft or credit fraud is to contact the credit bureaus and place a fraud alert on your credit report. This alert will notify potential creditors that your identity has been stolen or that your credit is being fraudulently used. You should also monitor your credit report regularly and dispute any fraudulent activity immediately.

If you have become a victim of identity theft or credit fraud, there are several steps you can take to protect your credit score and financial stability. One of the most important steps is to file a report with the Federal Trade Commission (FTC) and local law enforcement. You should also contact your creditors and financial institutions to report the fraud and freeze or close any accounts that have been compromised.

In addition to these steps, you may also want to consider signing up for credit monitoring services, which can alert you to any suspicious activity on your credit report. It is also a good idea to review your credit report regularly and dispute any errors or inaccuracies that could negatively impact your credit score.

In conclusion, identity theft and credit fraud are serious crimes that can have long-lasting effects on your credit score and financial stability. Being vigilant and proactive in detecting and preventing these crimes can help protect your credit and financial well-being. If you suspect that you have become a victim of identity theft or credit fraud, it is important to take action immediately to minimize the damage and restore your credit score.

CHAPTER 12: NEGOTIATING WITH CREDITORS

If you're struggling with debt, negotiating with creditors can be a helpful strategy to improve your credit score. Negotiating with creditors means you are attempting to settle your debt by paying less than the full amount owed. In this chapter, we will explore the basics of negotiating with creditors and how to get the best deals.

Before you start negotiating with creditors, it's important to understand that it may not always be possible to settle your debts for less than what you owe. However, it is worth trying to negotiate as it could save you money and help improve your credit score.

Here are some steps to take when negotiating with creditors:

Gather all relevant information: Before contacting your creditor, make sure you have all the relevant information, such as your account number, balance owed, and payment history. This will help you negotiate effectively and increase your chances of success.

Explain your situation: Be honest and explain your financial situation to your creditor. If you're struggling to make payments, they may be more willing to negotiate a settlement.

Offer a settlement: When negotiating with creditors, you should offer a settlement amount that you can afford. You could offer to pay a lump sum or agree to a payment plan over a set period.

Get the agreement in writing: If your creditor agrees to a settlement, make sure you get the agreement in writing. This will help you avoid any misunderstandings or disputes in the future.

Make the payment: Once you have agreed on a settlement, make sure you make the payment as agreed. This will help you avoid any further negative marks on your credit report.

Negotiating with creditors can be a challenging process, but it can also be very rewarding. It's important to be patient, persistent, and willing to compromise. Remember, the goal is to find a solution that works for both you and your creditor.

In some cases, it may be helpful to seek professional help when negotiating with creditors. Credit counseling agencies and debt settlement companies can help you negotiate with creditors and develop a plan to pay off your debts. However, it's important to choose a reputable service provider and be aware of any fees associated with their services.

In summary, negotiating with creditors can be an effective strategy to improve your credit score and reduce your debt. It's important to be prepared, honest, and persistent when negotiating with creditors. Seeking professional help can also be a helpful option in some cases.

CHAPTER 13: BUILDING CREDIT FROM SCRATCH

Building credit from scratch can seem daunting, but it is essential for establishing a good credit score. Without a credit history, it can be challenging to obtain loans or credit cards, and it can also impact your ability to rent an apartment or get a job.

Here are some steps you can take to build credit from scratch:

Get a secured credit card: A secured credit card requires a cash deposit as collateral and is an excellent option for building credit. Make sure to choose a secured card that reports to the major credit bureaus.

Become an authorized user: If someone you know has a good credit score, ask them to add you as an authorized user to their credit card account. This will allow you to build credit while still being responsible for your own spending.

Apply for a credit builder loan: A credit builder loan is a type of loan designed to help build credit. The lender will hold the funds in a savings account while you make regular payments. Once the loan is paid off, you will have built credit and have access to the funds.

Pay your bills on time: Even if your bills, such as rent or utilities, are not reported to the credit bureaus, paying them on time will help establish a history of responsible payments.

Keep your credit utilization low: If you do obtain a credit card, make sure to keep your credit utilization low. This means only using a small percentage of your available credit and paying off the balance in full each month.

Building credit from scratch takes time, but with patience and responsible financial habits, you can establish a good credit score and improve your financial future.

CHAPTER 14: CREDIT SCORE MYTHS AND MISCONCEPTIONS

Credit scores are a crucial part of financial well-being, but there is a lot of misinformation floating around about them. This chapter will debunk some of the most common credit score myths and misconceptions.

Myth #1: Checking Your Credit Score Will Hurt Your Score

This myth is entirely false. Checking your own credit score will not harm your credit score in any way. In fact, checking your credit score regularly is an essential part of maintaining good credit.

Myth #2: Closing Old Credit Accounts Will Improve Your Credit Score

This myth is partially true but can be misleading. Closing old credit accounts can actually harm your credit score if they have a long credit history and good payment history. When you close an old credit account, you reduce your overall available credit, which can increase your credit utilization rate, negatively affecting your credit score.

Myth #3: Only Debt Payment History Matters for Your Credit Score

While debt payment history is a significant factor in determining your credit score, it's not the only factor. Credit utilization rate, length of credit history, credit mix, and new credit inquiries also play a role in determining your credit score.

Myth #4: Paying Off Collections Will Improve Your Credit Score

Paying off collections will not remove them from your credit report or improve your credit score. Instead, they will be marked as "paid collections" on your credit report, which is still a negative item that can remain on your report for up to seven years.

Myth #5: You Can't Improve Your Credit Score if You Have a Bankruptcy or Foreclosure

While a bankruptcy or foreclosure can significantly harm your credit score, it's not the end of the world. You can still take steps to improve your credit score, such as paying your bills on time, reducing your credit utilization rate, and maintaining a good mix of credit.

Myth #6: Credit Repair Services Are a Scam

While there are some fraudulent credit repair companies out there, there are also reputable companies that can help you repair your credit. It's essential to do your research and choose a legitimate company that has a track record of success.

It's crucial to understand credit score myths and misconceptions to make informed financial decisions. By knowing the truth about credit scores, you can take steps to improve your credit score and avoid common mistakes that can negatively impact it.

CHAPTER 15: THE FUTURE OF CREDIT REPAIR

The credit repair industry is always changing and evolving to meet the needs of consumers. In the past few years, there have been significant advancements in technology, new regulations, and consumer trends that are shaping the future of credit repair.

One significant development is the increasing use of artificial intelligence (AI) and machine learning in the credit repair process. AI-powered software can analyze vast amounts of data and identify patterns that human analysts might miss, making the credit repair process more efficient and effective.

Another trend in the credit repair industry is the increased focus on financial education and coaching. Rather than just fixing credit reports, many credit repair services are now providing educational resources and personalized coaching to help consumers improve their financial literacy and make better financial decisions.

Furthermore, regulatory changes, such as the Credit Repair Organizations Act (CROA), have put more pressure on credit repair companies to operate ethically and transparently. This has led to the emergence of more reputable and trustworthy credit repair companies that prioritize the needs of their clients.

Finally, consumer trends such as the increased use of mobile technology and the desire for greater transparency and control over personal data are also shaping the future of credit repair. Credit repair companies that offer mobile apps, online portals, and real-time updates are becoming increasingly popular, as consumers look for more convenient and user-friendly ways to track their credit repair progress.

In conclusion, the future of credit repair is exciting and promising, with advances in technology, regulations, and consumer trends shaping the industry. As credit repair companies continue to evolve and adapt to these changes, consumers can expect more efficient, effective, and transparent credit repair services in the years to come.

www.ingramcontent.com/pod-product-compliance
Lightning Source LLC
Chambersburg PA
CBHW051719250726

48653CB00008B/3117